THE BEATLES
BANJO TAB

Arranged by Mark Phillips

Cover photo by CBS Photo Archive / Getty Images

ISBN 978-1-4803-9305-9

HAL•LEONARD®
CORPORATION
7777 W. BLUEMOUND RD. P.O. BOX 13819 MILWAUKEE, WI 53213

Visit Hal Leonard Online at
www.halleonard.com

All My Loving

Words and Music by John Lennon and Paul McCartney

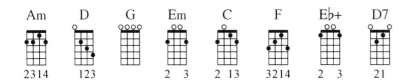

Key of G

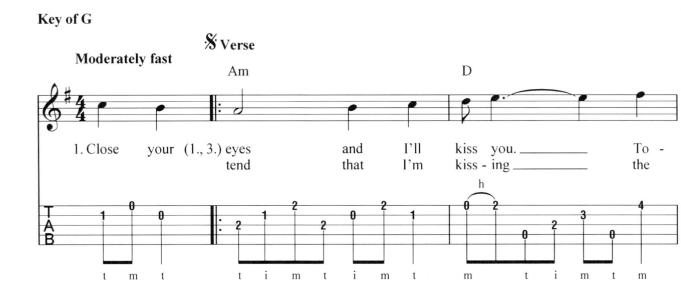

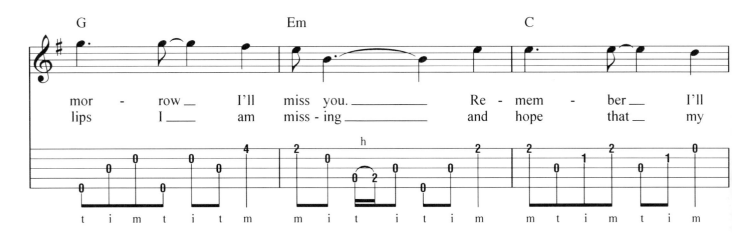

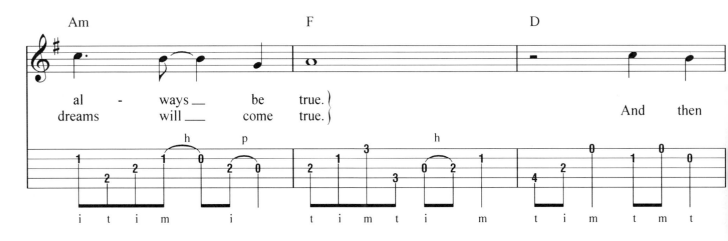

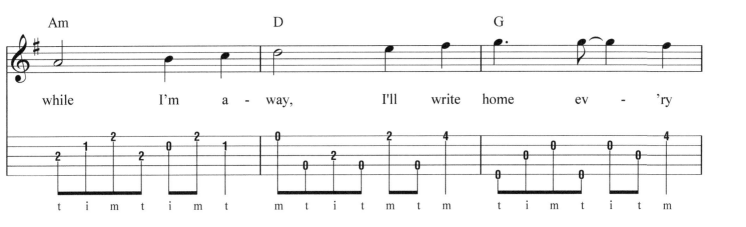

while I'm a - way, I'll write home ev - 'ry

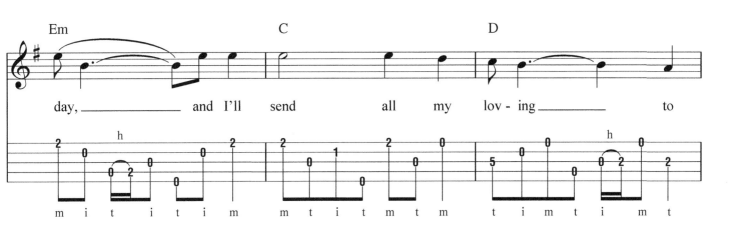

day, _____ and I'll send all my lov - ing _____ to

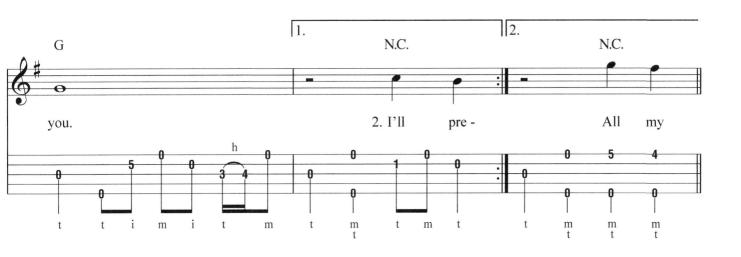

you.   2. I'll pre -   All my

Bridge

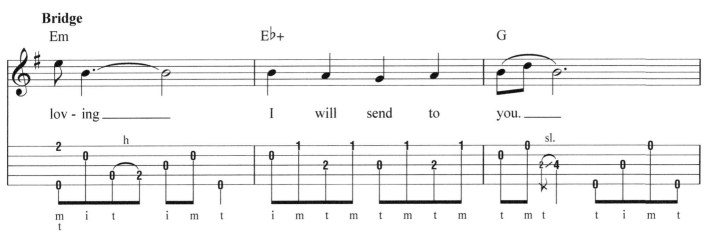

lov - ing _____   I will send to you. _____

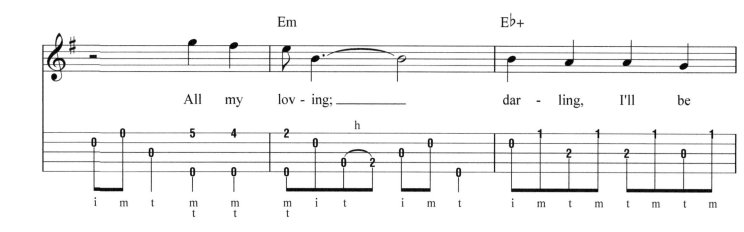

All my lov - ing; _____ dar - ling, I'll be

To Coda ⊕   **Interlude**

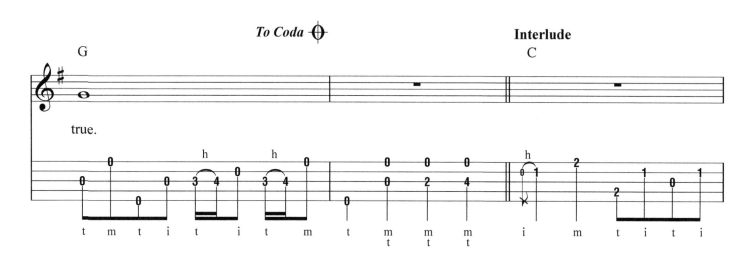

true.

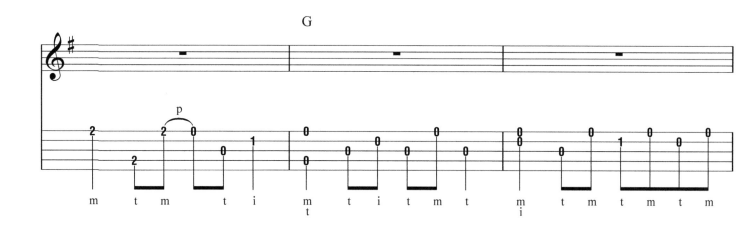

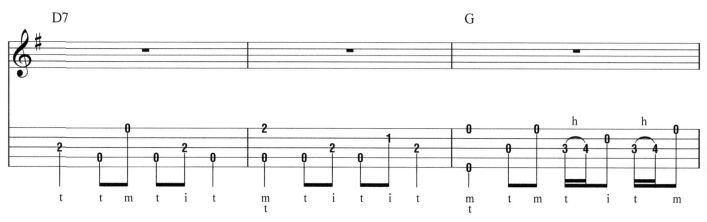

Can't Buy Me Love

Words and Music by John Lennon and Paul McCartney

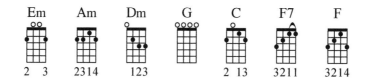

Key of C

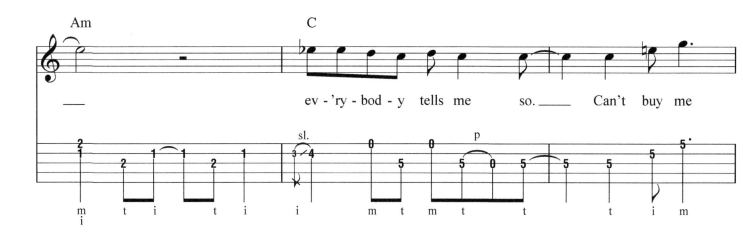

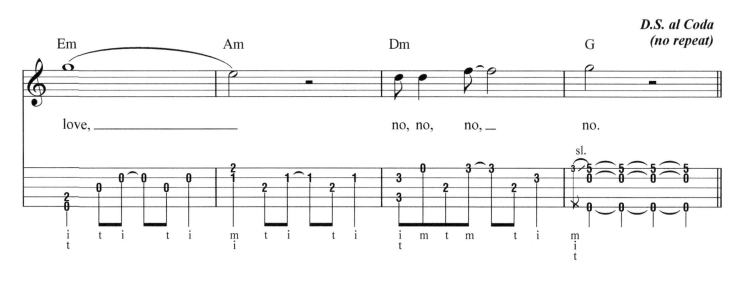

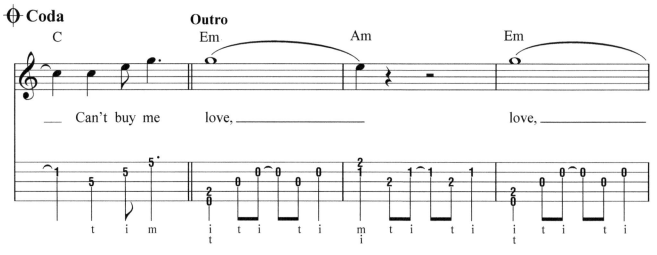

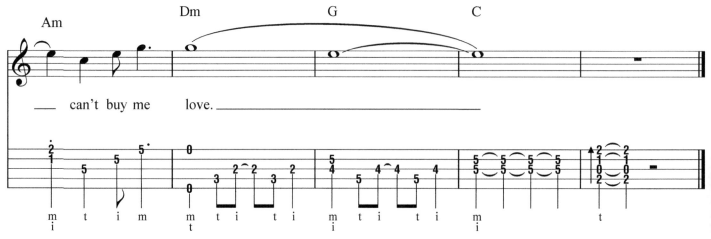

Come Together

Words and Music by John Lennon and Paul McCartney

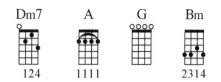

Key of D minor

Intro
Moderately

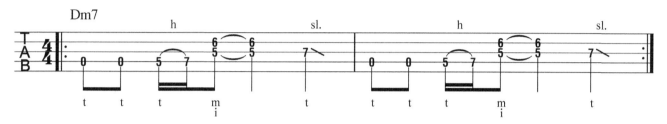

Verse

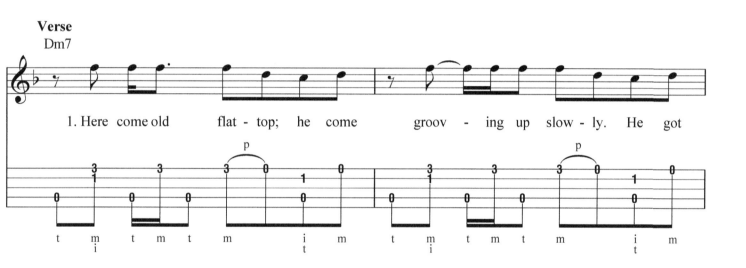

1. Here come old flat-top; he come groov-ing up slow-ly. He got

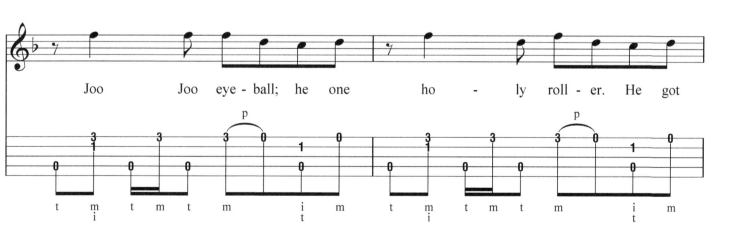

Joo Joo eye-ball; he one ho-ly roll-er. He got

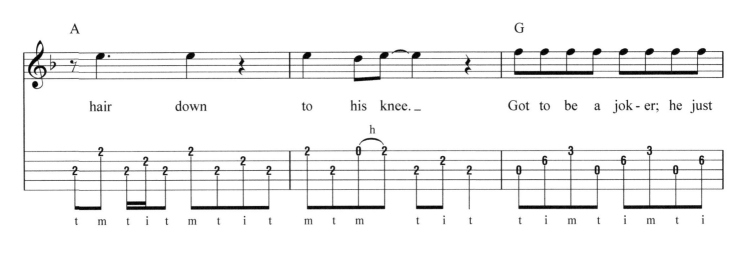

hair down to his knee. _ Got to be a jok - er; he just

Interlude

Dm7

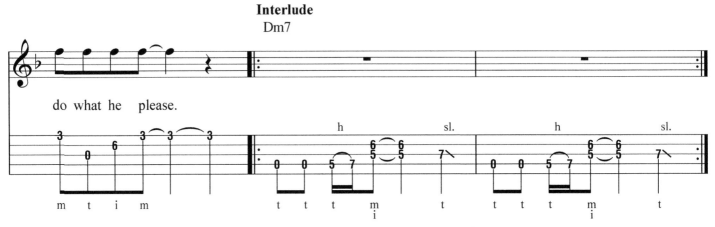

do what he please.

Verse

Dm7

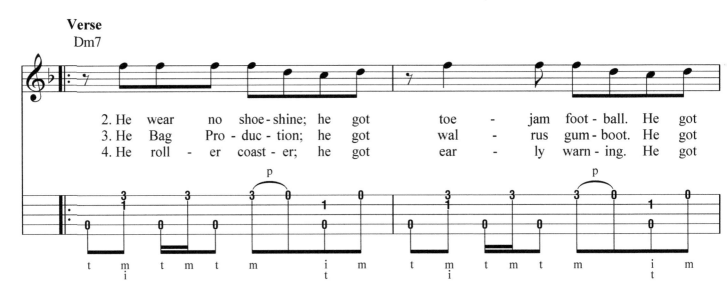

2. He wear no shoe - shine; he got toe - jam foot - ball. He got
3. He Bag Pro - duc - tion; he got wal - rus gum - boot. He got
4. He roll - er coast - er; he got ear - ly warn - ing. He got

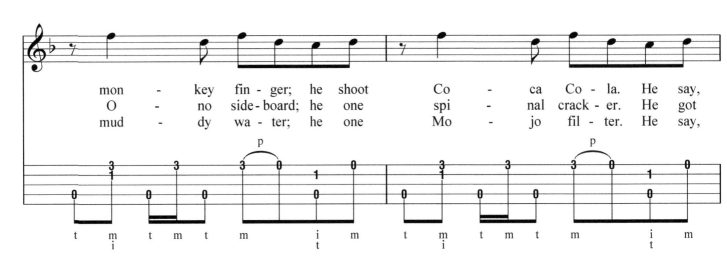

mon - key fin - ger; he shoot Co - ca Co - la. He say,
O - no side - board; he one spi - nal crack - er. He got
mud - dy wa - ter; he one Mo - jo fil - ter. He say,

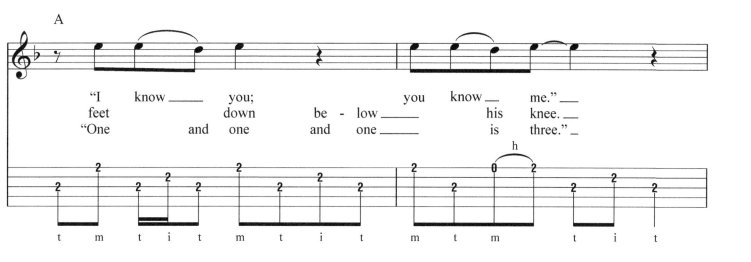

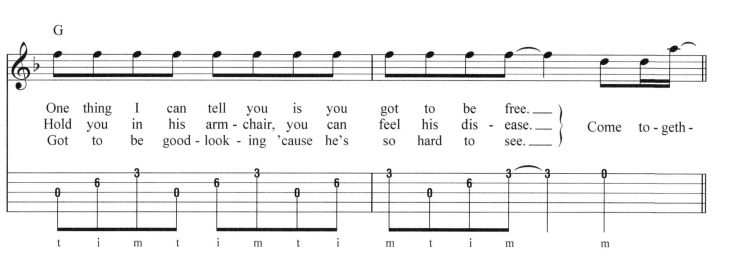

Chorus   **Interlude/Outro**

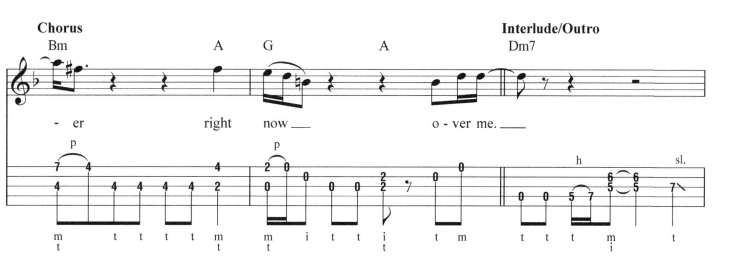

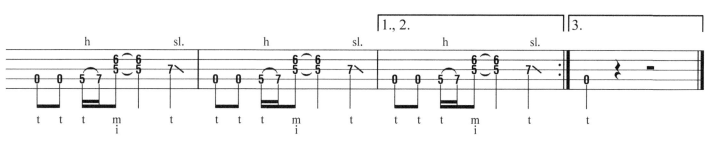

Day Tripper

Words and Music by John Lennon and Paul McCartney

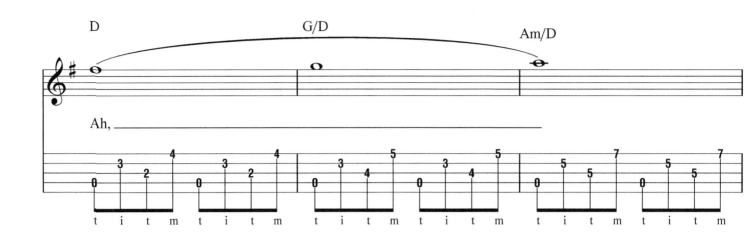

D.C. al Coda
(no repeat)

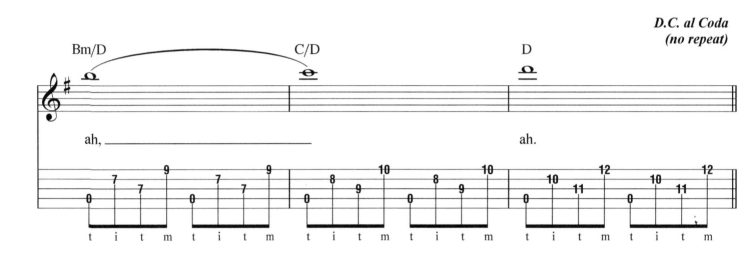

✛ **Coda**

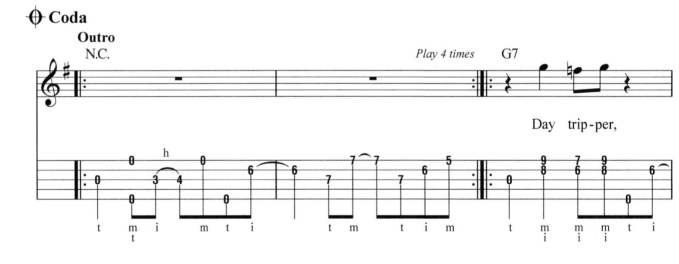

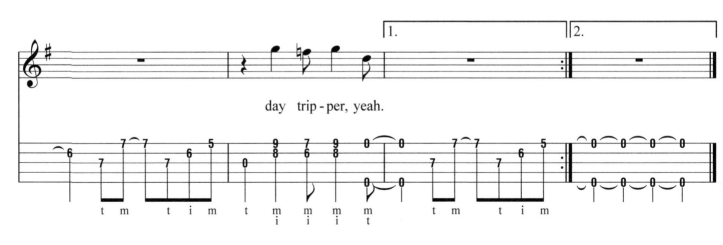

Eleanor Rigby

Words and Music by John Lennon and Paul McCartney

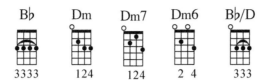

Key of D minor

Intro
Moderately

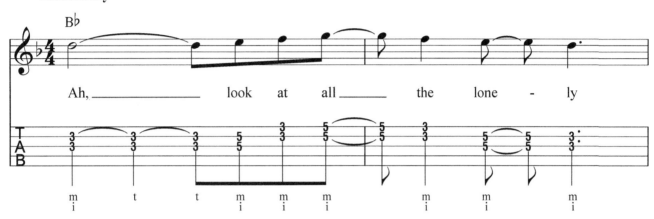

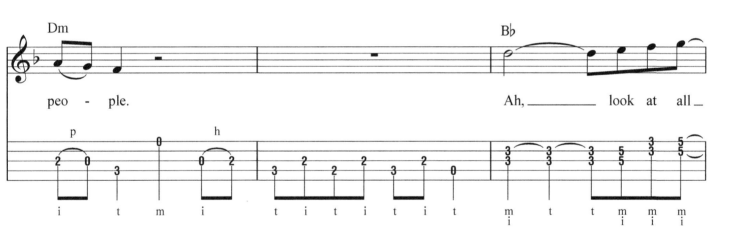

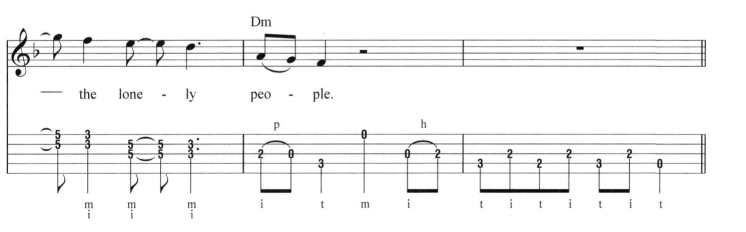

Verse

1. El - ea - nor Rig - by   picks up the rice ___ in the church ___
2. Fa - ther Mc - Ken - zie   writ - ing the words ___ of a ser -
3. El - ea - nor Rig - by   died in the church ___ and was bur -

— where a wed - ding has been; ___
— mon that no ___ one will hear; ___
— ied a - long ___ with her name; ___

lives in a dream. ___   Waits at the win - dow,
no one comes near. ___   Look at him work - ing,
no - bod - y came. ___   Fa - ther Mc - Ken - zie,

wear - ing the face ___ that she keeps ___ in a jar ___ by the door. ___
darn - ing his socks ___ in the night ___ when there's no - bod - y there. ___
wip - ing the dirt ___ from his hands ___ as he walks ___ from the grave; ___

I Want to Hold Your Hand

Words and Music by John Lennon and Paul McCartney

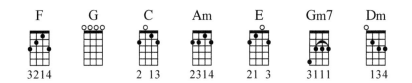

Key of C

Intro
Moderately

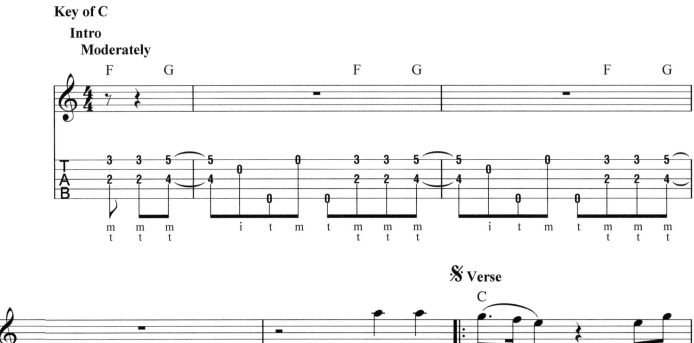

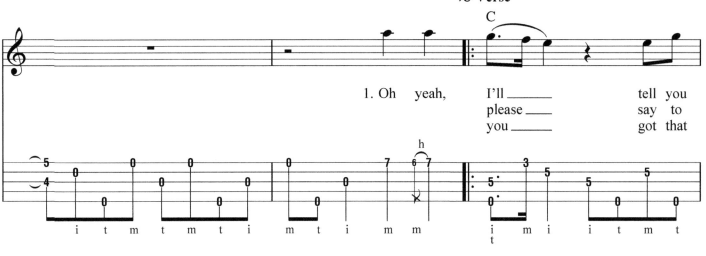

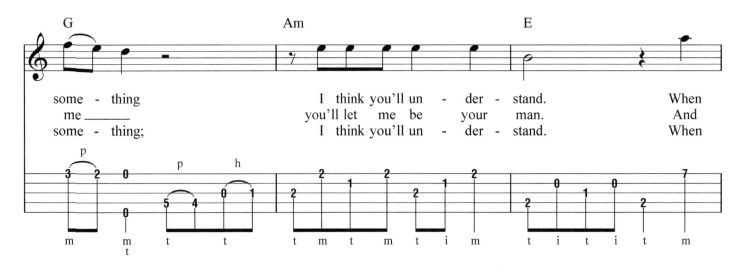

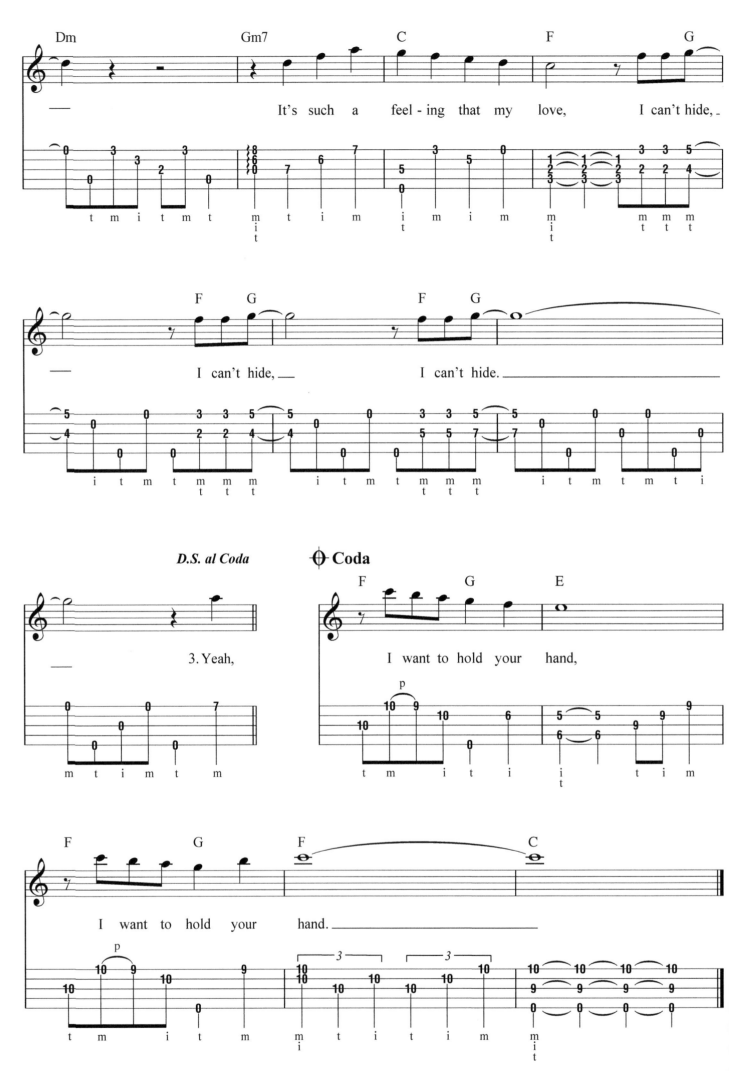

Here, There and Everywhere

Words and Music by John Lennon and Paul McCartney

No - bod - y can de - ny that there's some - thing there.
Some - one is speak - ing but she does - n't know he's there.

Bridge

I want her ev - 'ry - where, and if she's be - side me I know I need

nev - er care. 3., 4. But to love her is to need her

Verse

ev - 'ry - where, know - ing that love is to share,

I Will

Words and Music by John Lennon and Paul McCartney

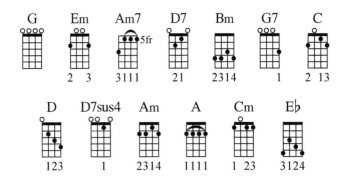

Key of G

Verse

Moderately

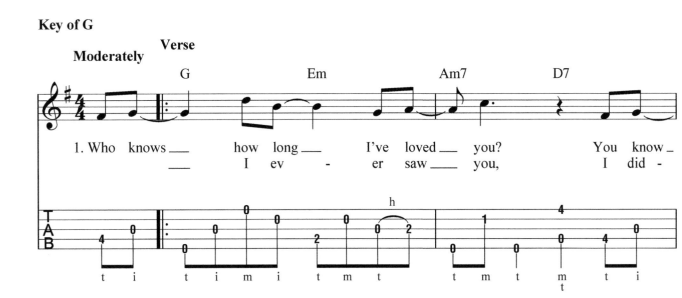

1. Who knows __ how long __ I've loved __ you? You know __
__ I ev - er saw __ you, I did -

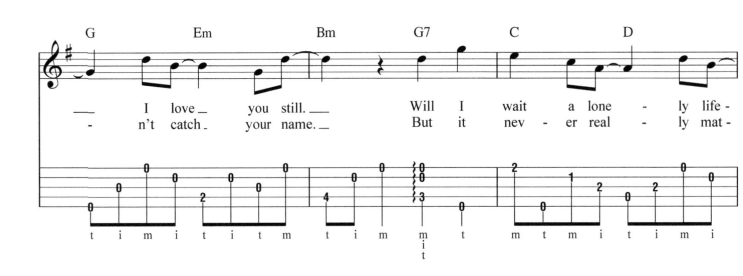

__ I love __ you still. __ Will I wait a lone - ly life
- n't catch __ your name. __ But it nev - er real - ly mat -

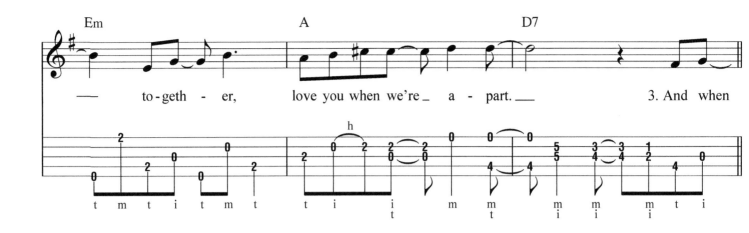

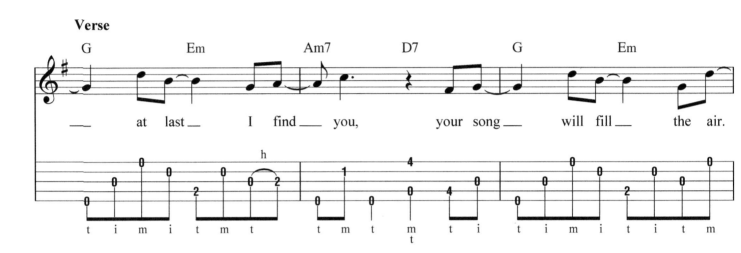

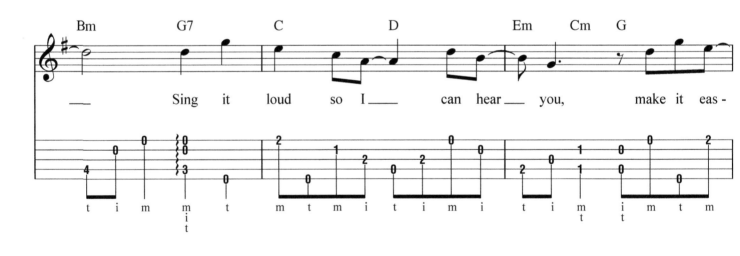

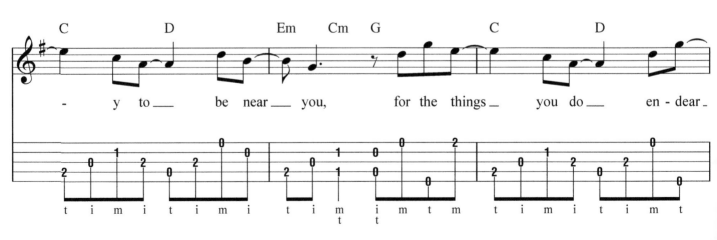

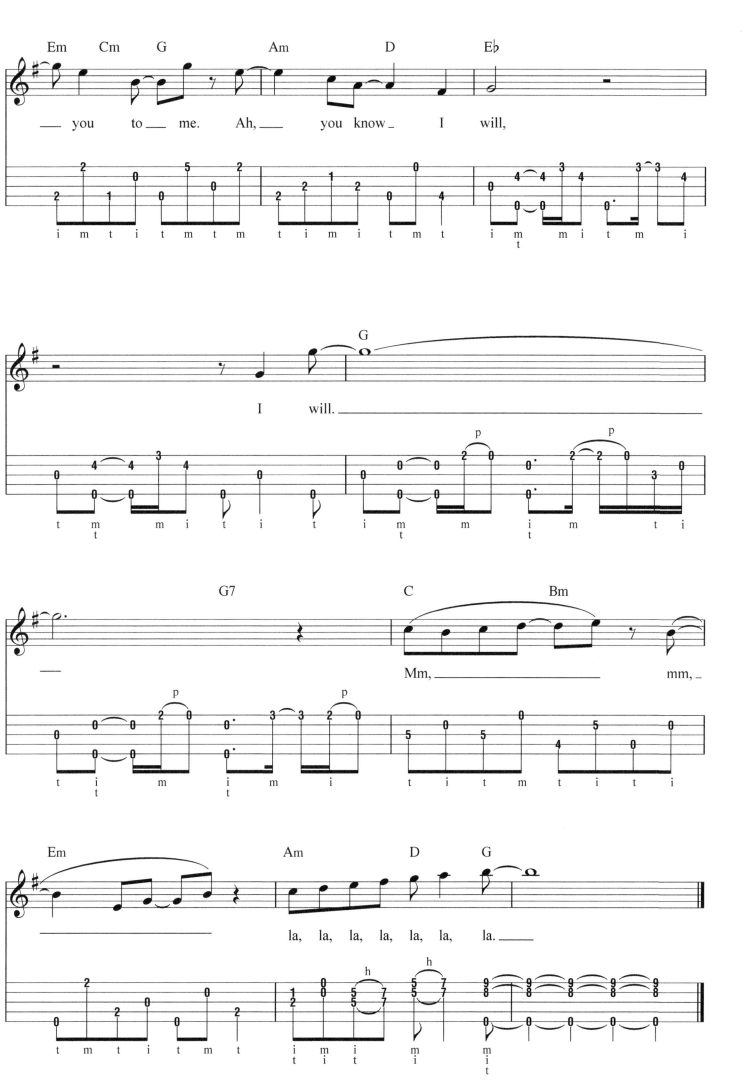

Let It Be

Words and Music by John Lennon and Paul McCartney

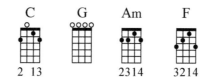

Key of C

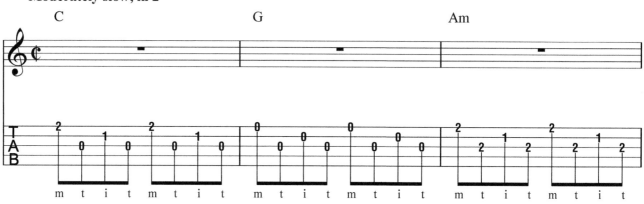

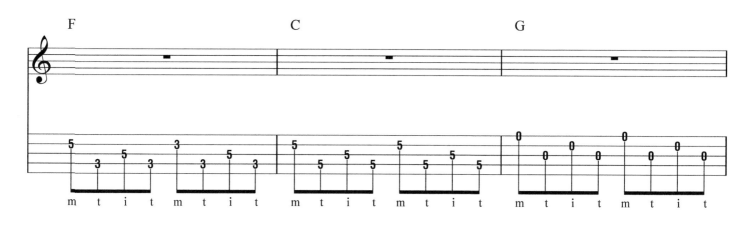

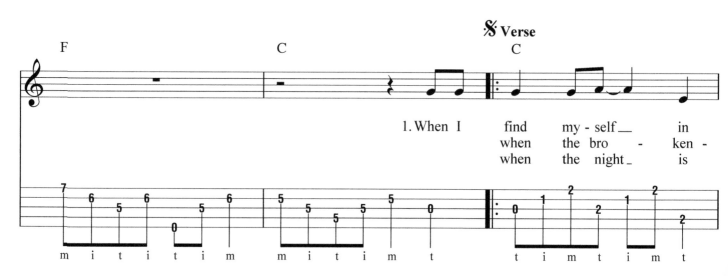

Ob-La-Di, Ob-La-Da

Words and Music by John Lennon and Paul McCartney

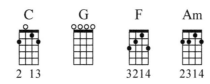

Key of C

Verse
Moderately

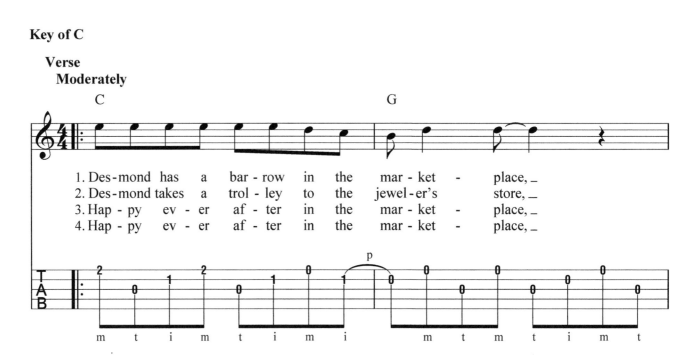

1. Des-mond has a bar-row in the mar-ket - place, _
2. Des-mond takes a trol-ley to the jewel-er's store, _
3. Hap-py ev-er af-ter in the mar-ket - place, _
4. Hap-py ev-er af-ter in the mar-ket - place, _

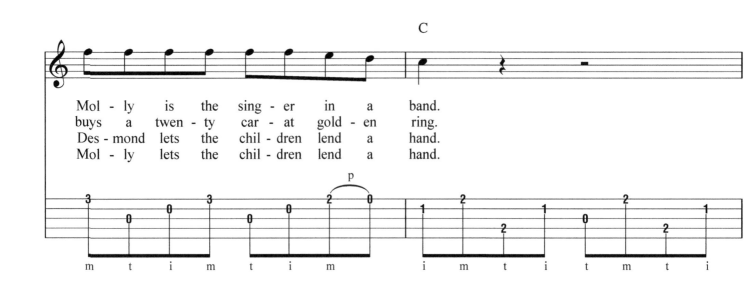

Mol-ly is the sing-er in a band.
buys a twen-ty car-at gold-en ring.
Des-mond lets the chil-dren lend a hand.
Mol-ly lets the chil-dren lend a hand.

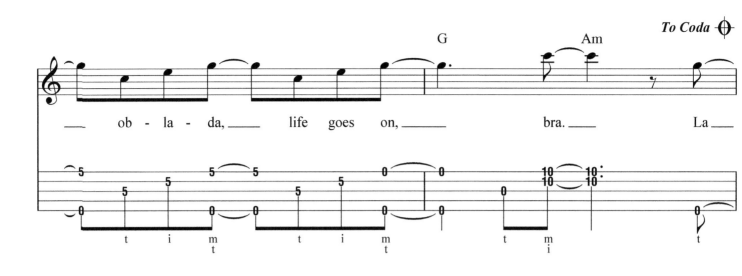

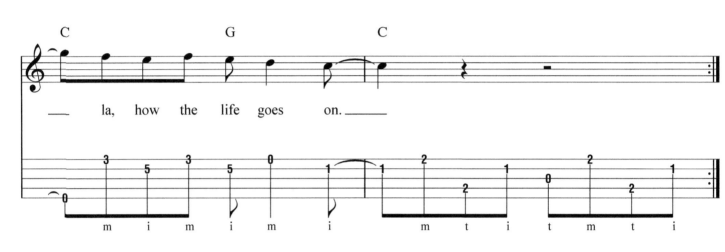

Bridge

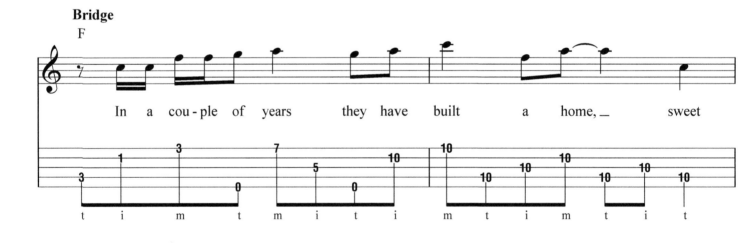

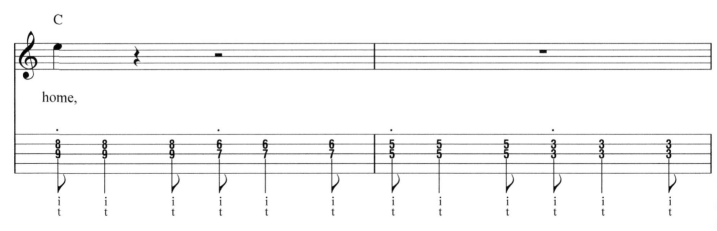

Penny Lane

Words and Music by John Lennon and Paul McCartney

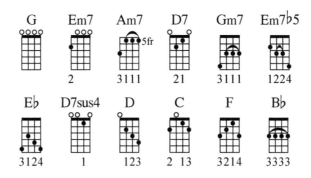

Key of G

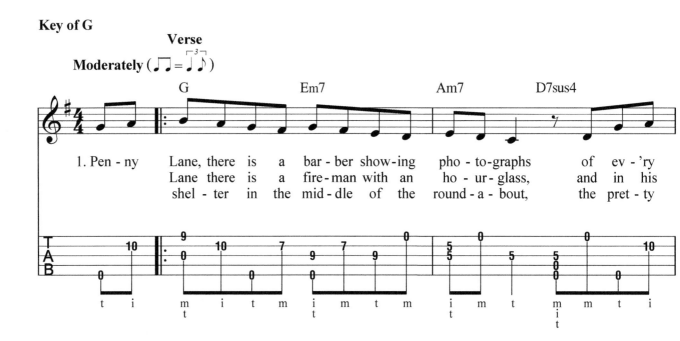

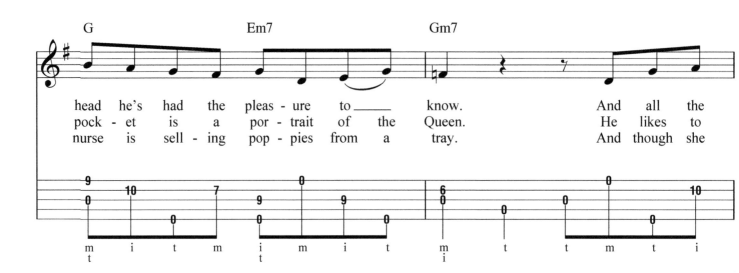

Something

Words and Music by George Harrison

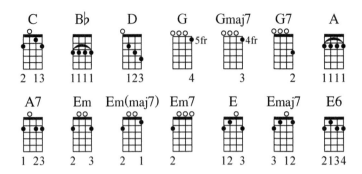

Key of G

Intro

Moderately slow, in 2

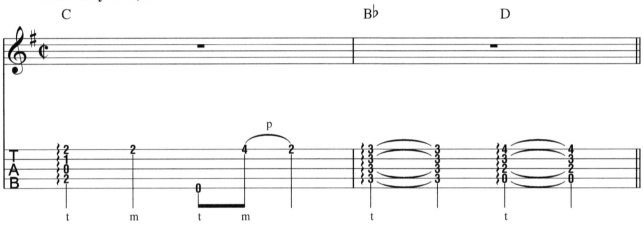

Verse

1. Some - thing in _____ the way _____ she
2. Some - where in _____ her smile _____ she
3. Some - thing in _____ the way _____ she

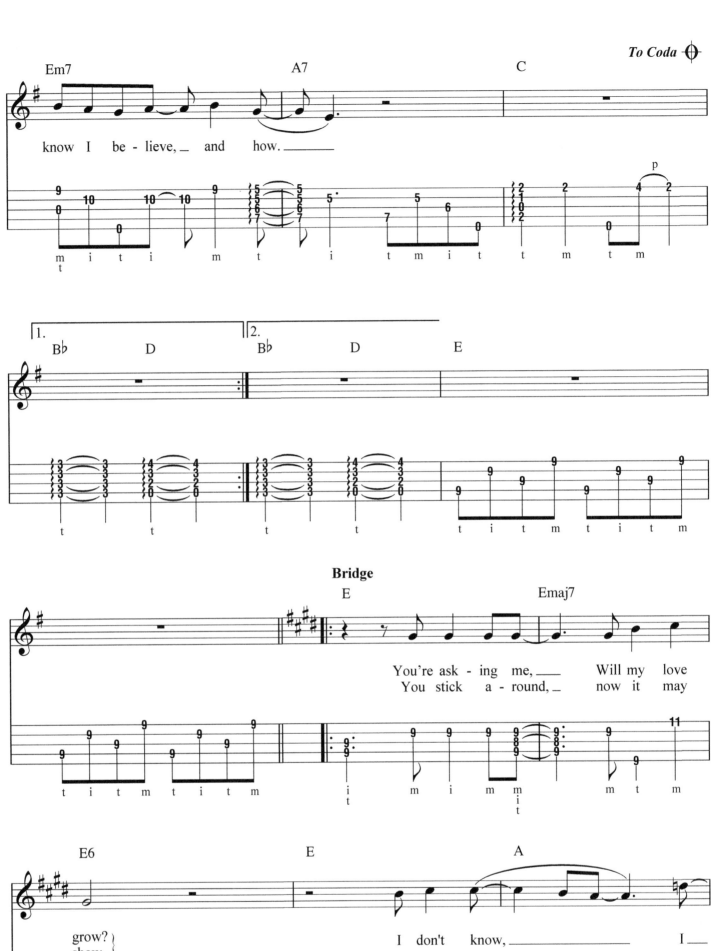

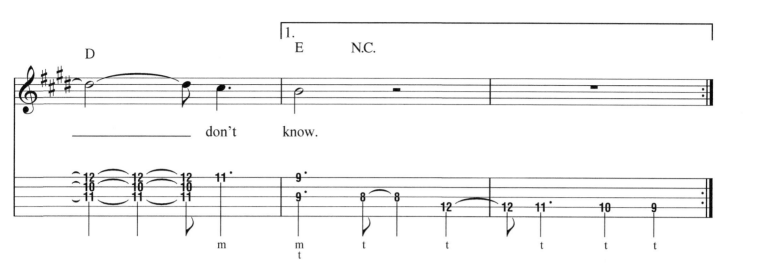

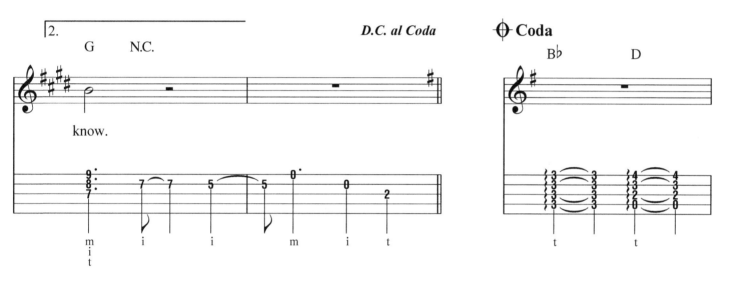

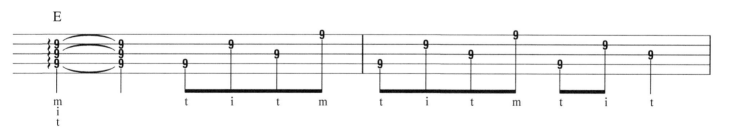

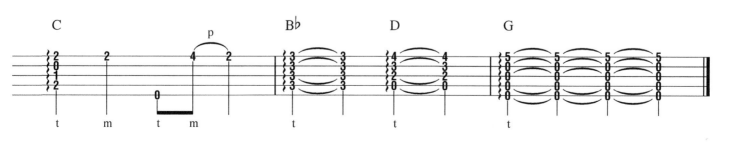

We Can Work It Out

Words and Music by John Lennon and Paul McCartney

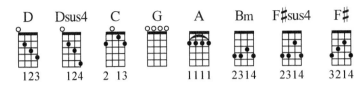

Key of D

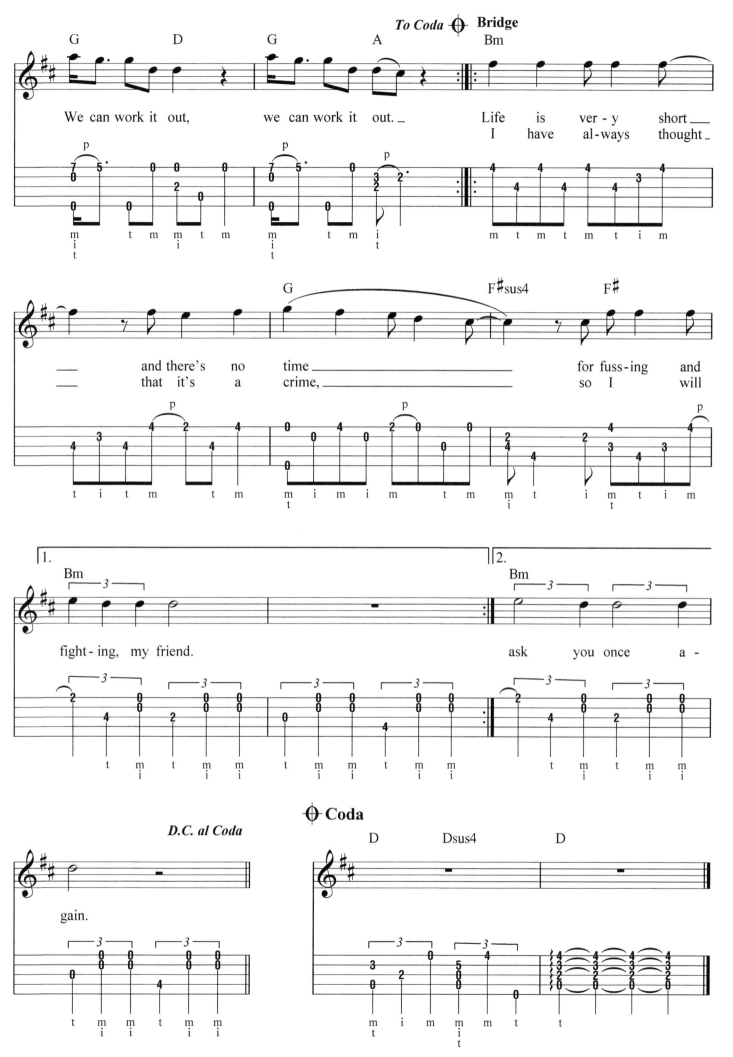

While My Guitar Gently Weeps

Words and Music by George Harrison

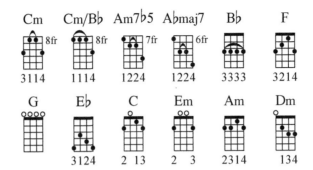

Key of C minor

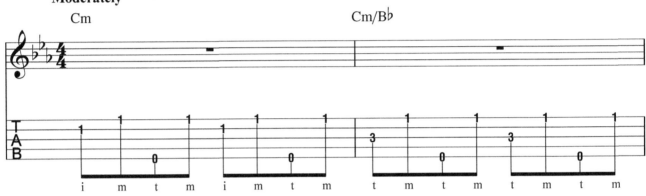

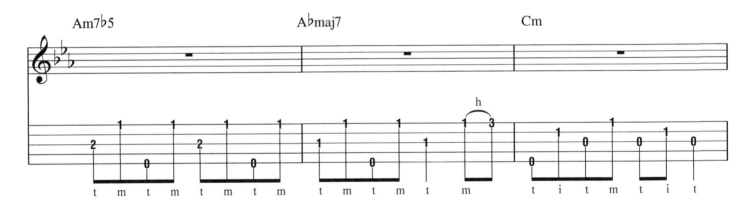

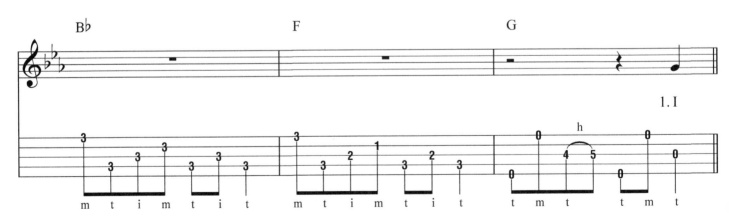

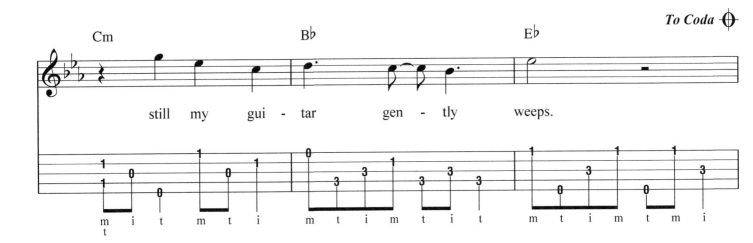

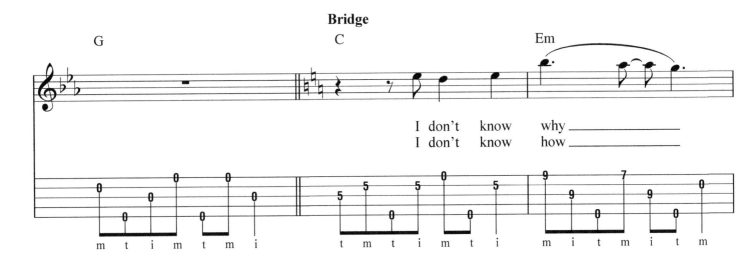

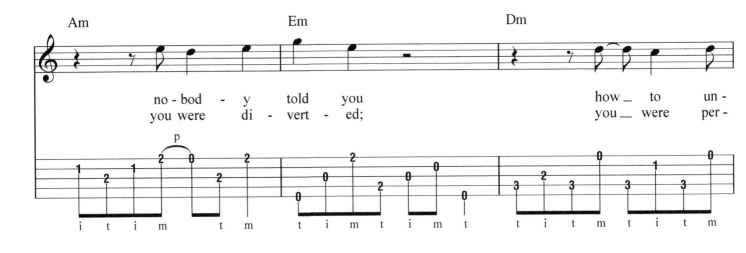

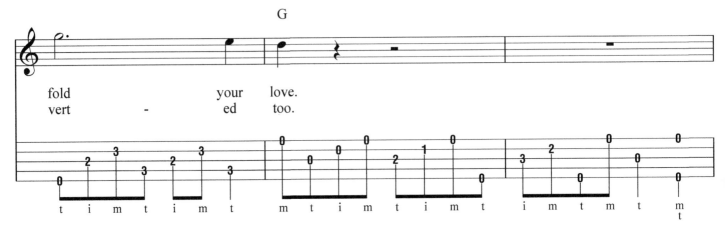

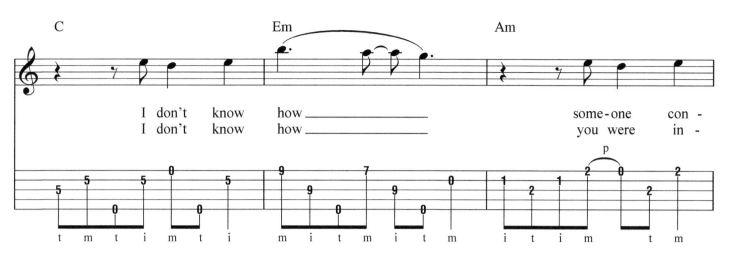

I don't know how _____ some-one con -
I don't know how _____ you were in -

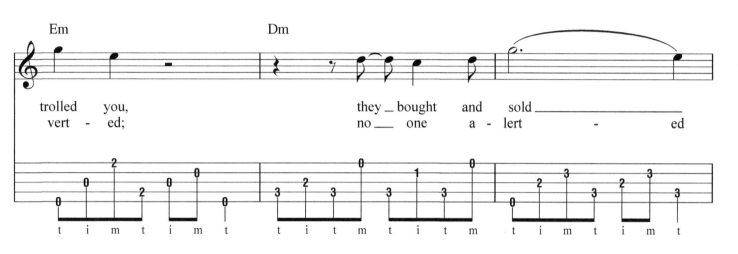

trolled you, they — bought and sold _____
vert - ed; no __ one a - lert - ed

2nd time, D.S. al Coda

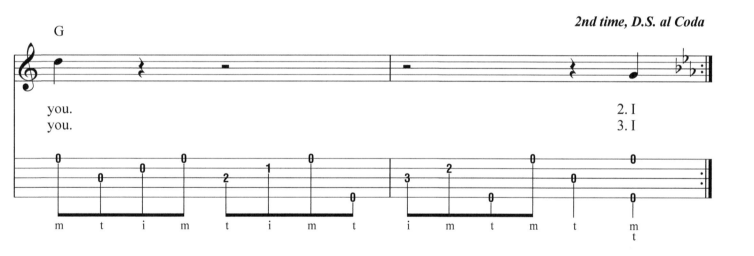

you.   2. I
you.   3. I

Coda

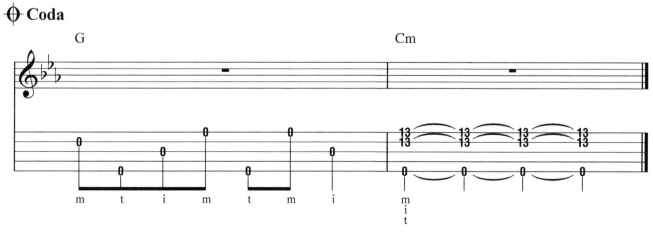

With a Little Help from My Friends

Words and Music by John Lennon and Paul McCartney

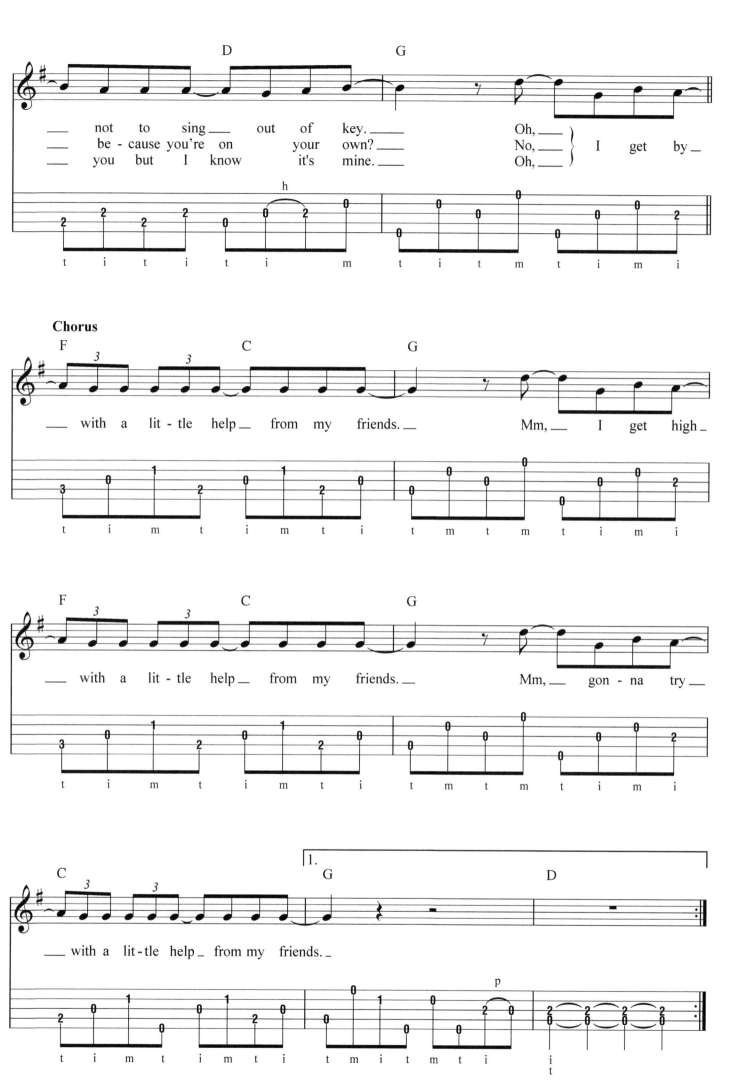

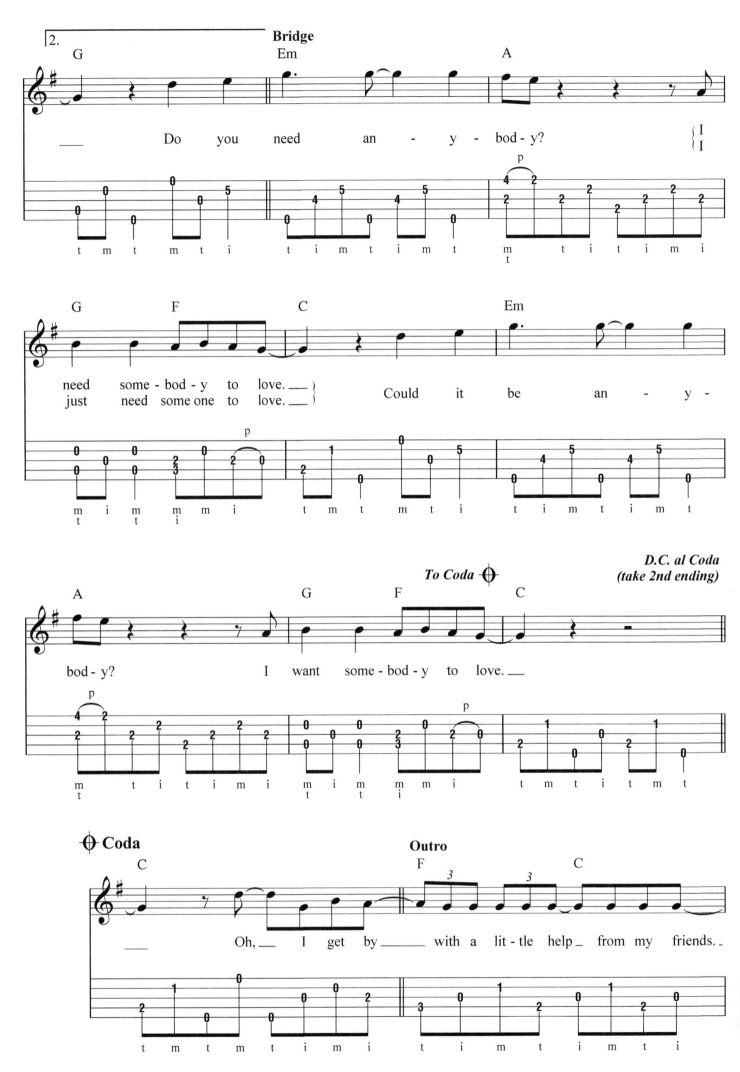

52

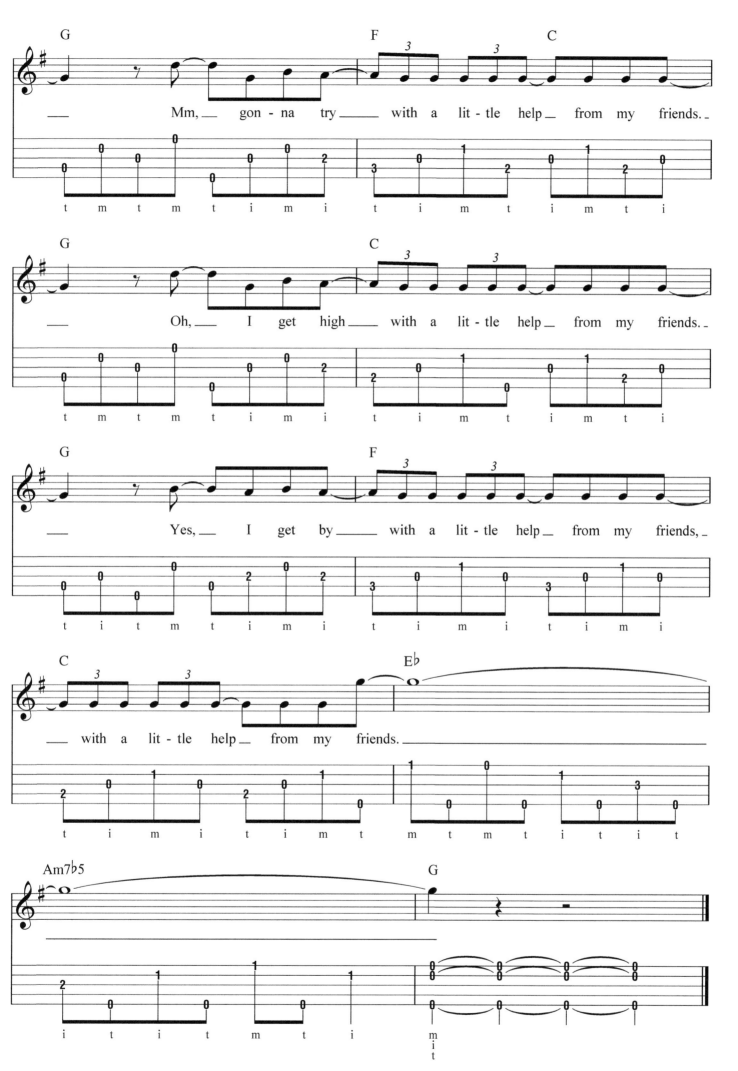

Yesterday

Words and Music by John Lennon and Paul McCartney

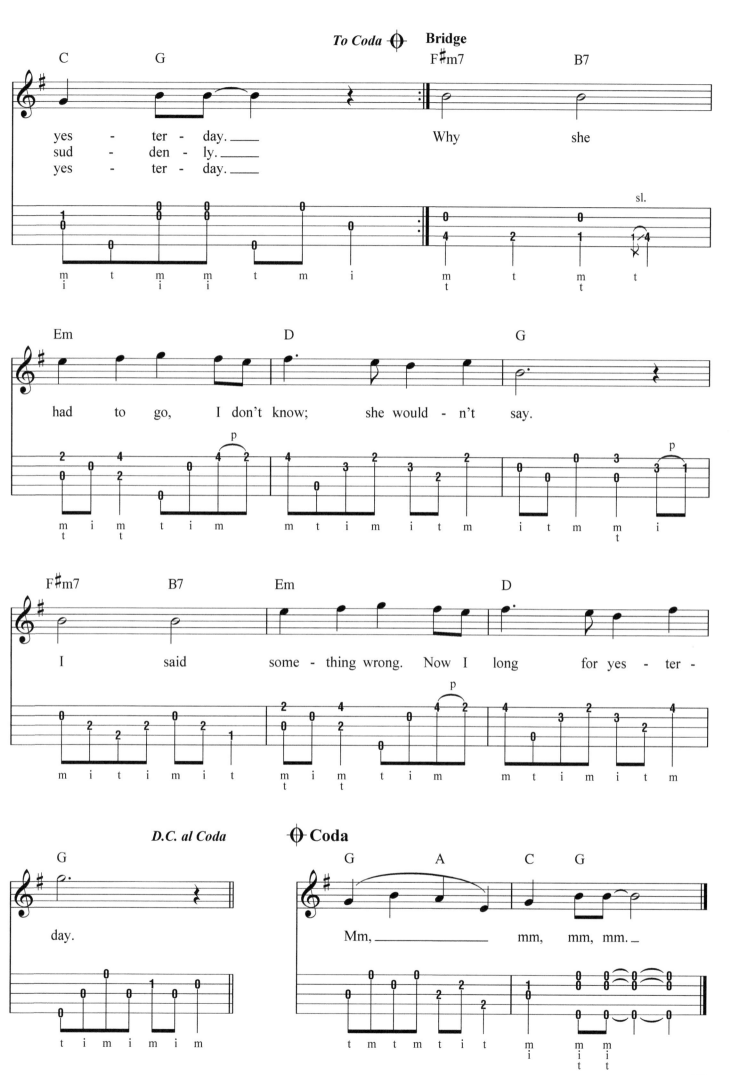

To Coda
Bridge
C G F♯m7 B7
yes - ter - day.
sud - den - ly.
yes - ter - day.
Why she
sl.
Em D G
had to go, I don't know; she would - n't say.
p
F♯m7 B7 Em D
I said some - thing wrong. Now I long for yes - ter -
D.C. al Coda
Coda
G
day.
G A C G
Mm, mm, mm, mm.

Yellow Submarine

Words and Music by John Lennon and Paul McCartney

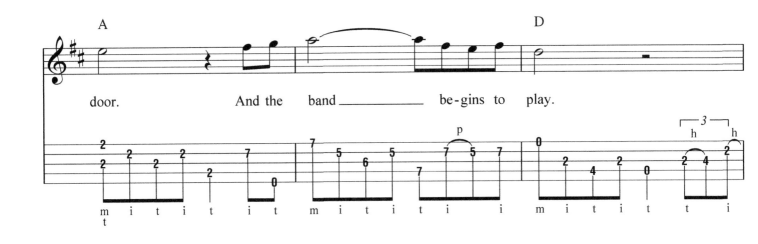

door. And the band _____ be-gins to play.

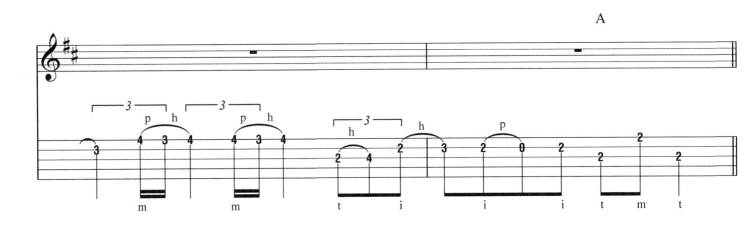

Chorus

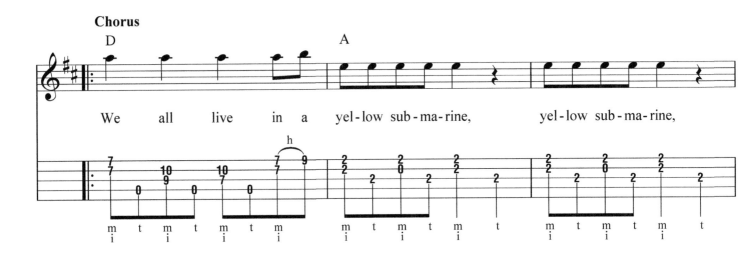

We all live in a yel-low sub-ma-rine, yel-low sub-ma-rine,

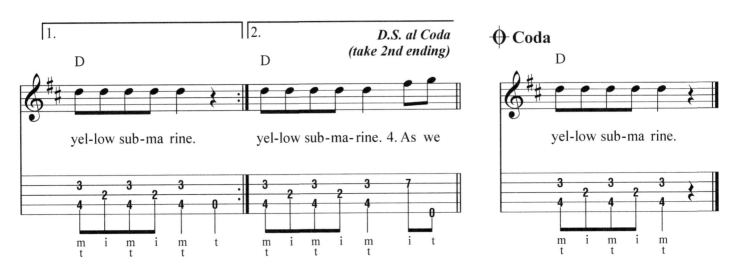

yel-low sub-ma rine. yel-low sub-ma-rine. 4. As we yel-low sub-ma rine.

Lady Madonna

Words and Music by John Lennon and Paul McCartney

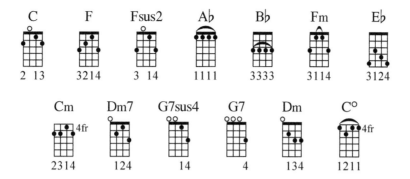

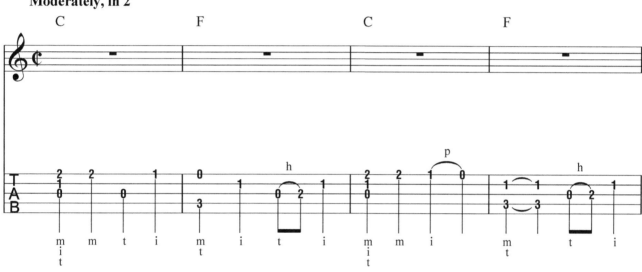

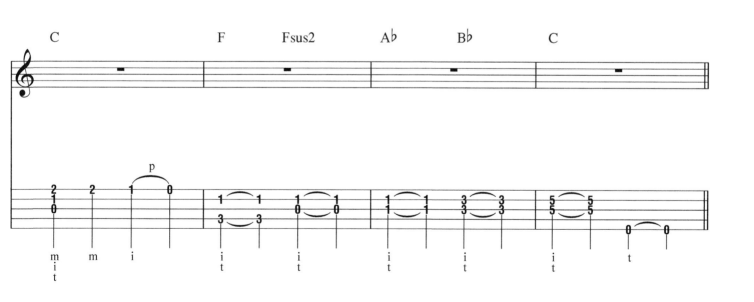

To Coda 2

Verse

3. La - dy Ma - don - na, ba - by at your breast,
4. La - dy Ma - don - na, ly - ing on the bed.

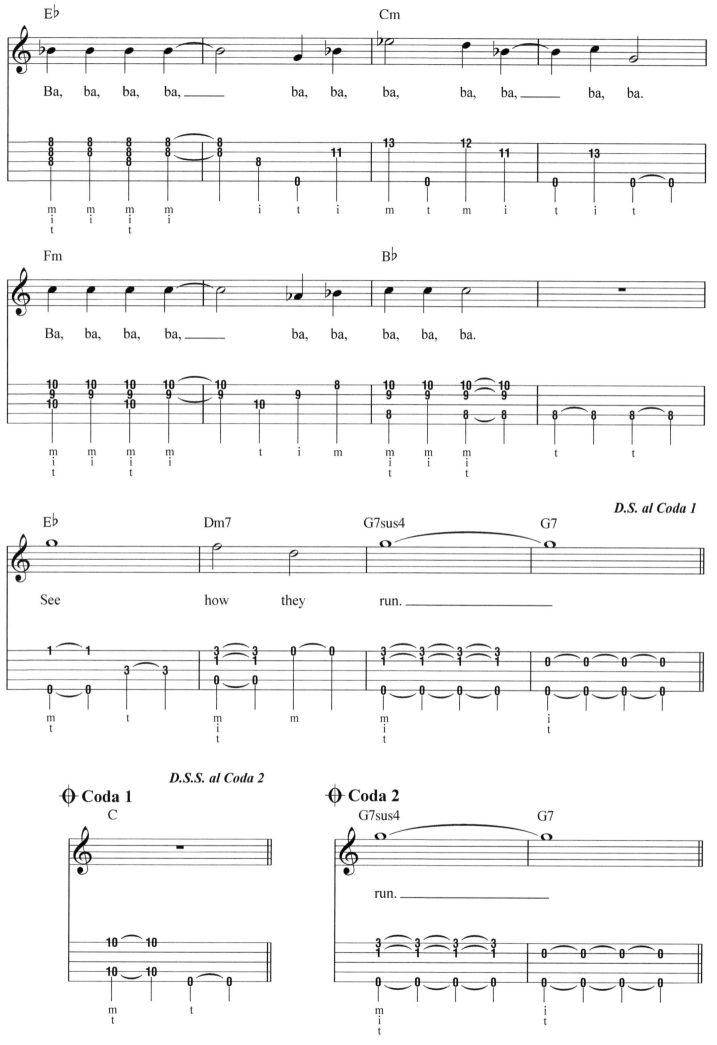

Love Me Do

Words and Music by John Lennon and Paul McCartney

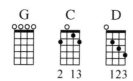

Key of G

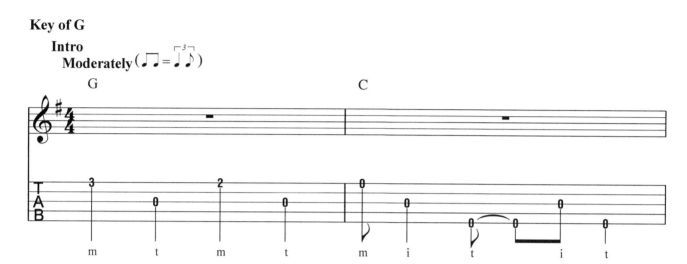

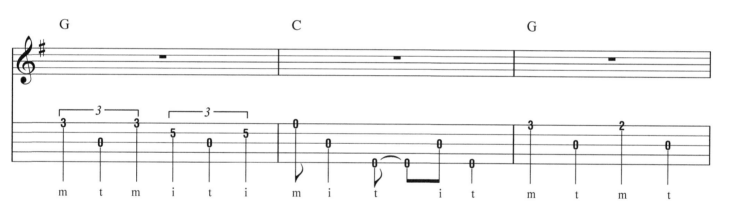

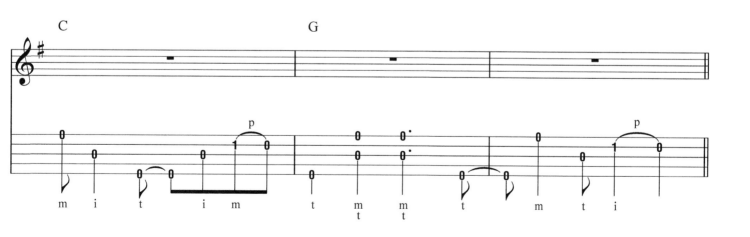

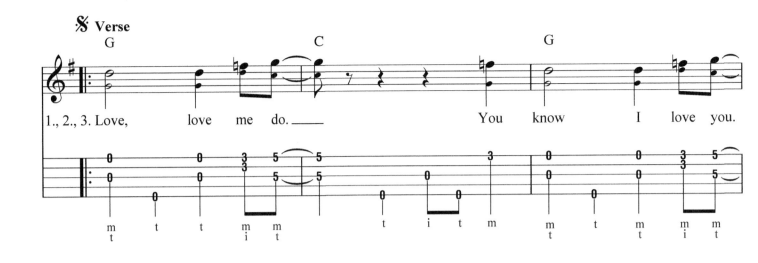

Verse

1., 2., 3. Love, love me do. ___ You know I love you.

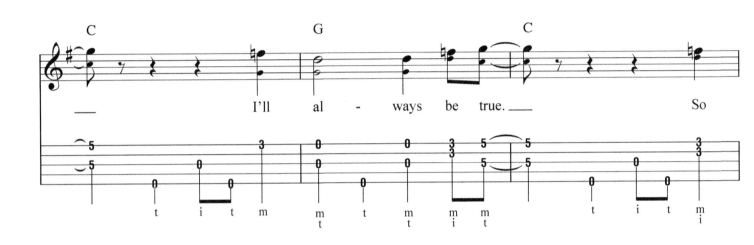

___ I'll al - ways be true. ___ So

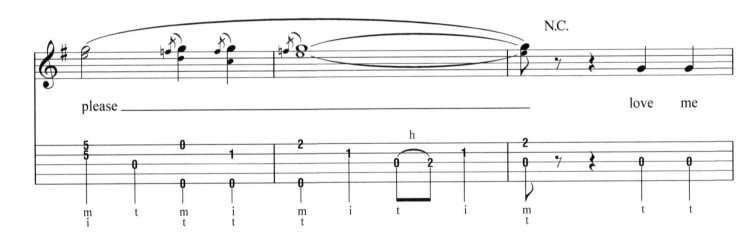

please ___ love me

To Coda

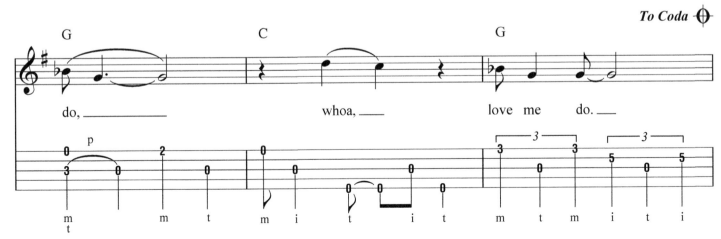

do, ___ whoa, ___ love me do. ___

Michelle

Words and Music by John Lennon and Paul McCartney

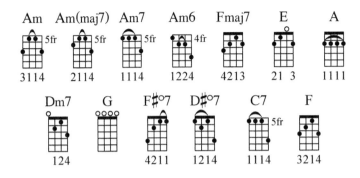

Key of A

Intro
Moderately slow, in 2

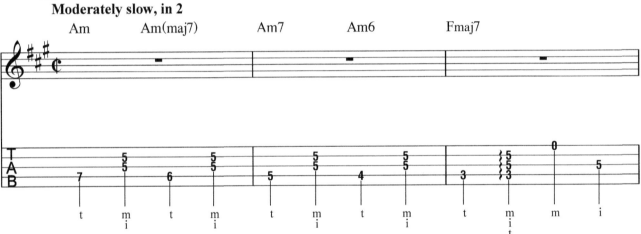

Verse

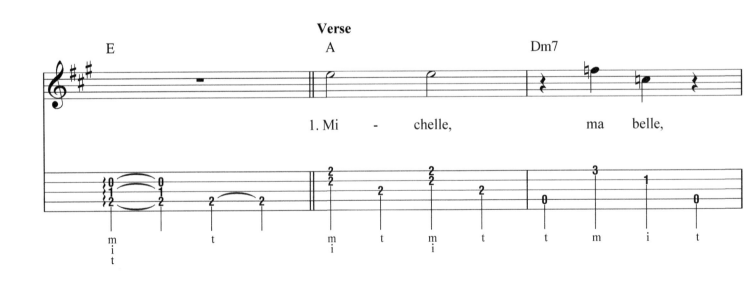

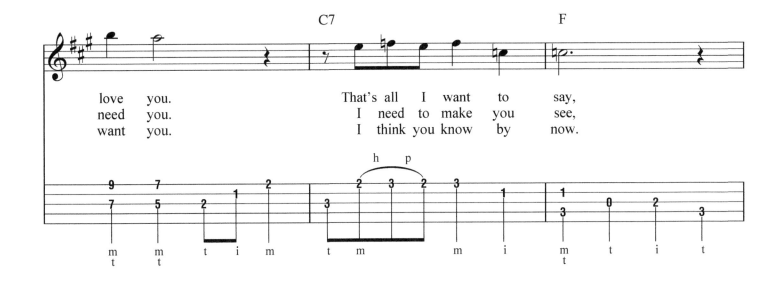

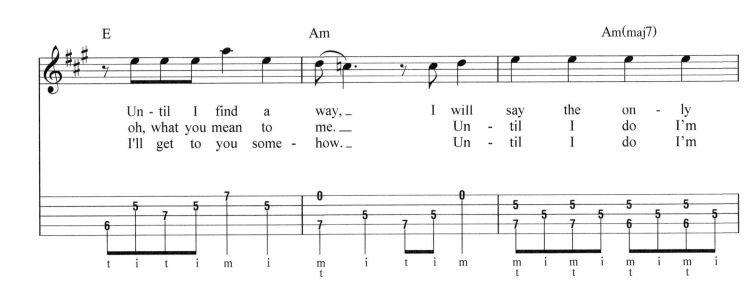

To Coda ⊕

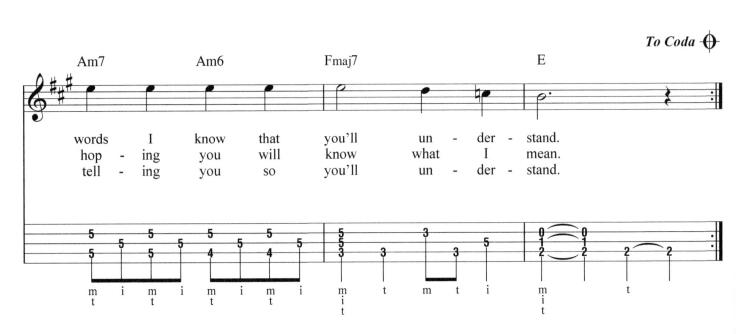

Interlude

I love ___ you. ___

D.S. al Coda
(no repeat)

I

⊕ Coda

Verse

4. Mi - chelle, ma belle, sont les mots qui

vont très bien en - semble, très bien en - semble. I will

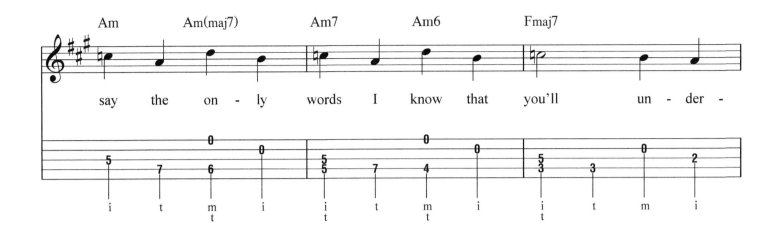

say the on - ly words I know that you'll un - der -

Outro

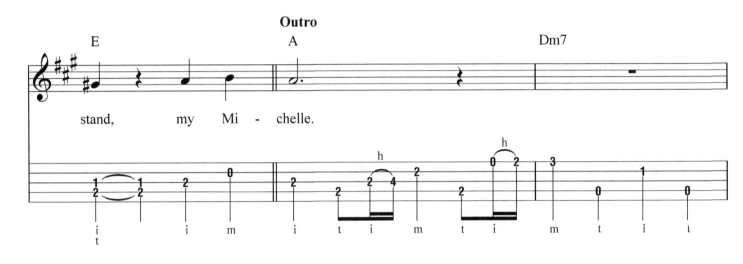

stand, my Mi - chelle.

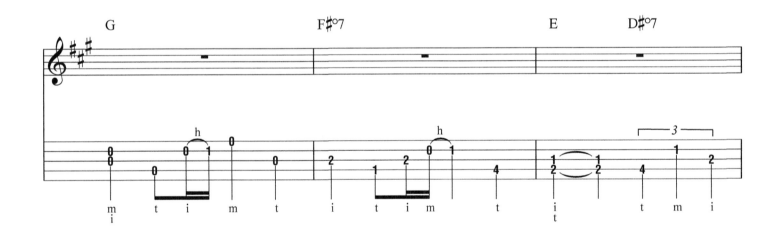

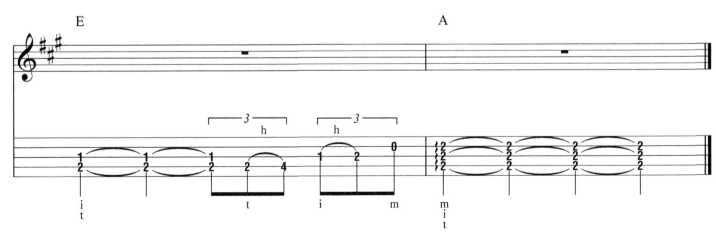

Paperback Writer

Words and Music by John Lennon and Paul McCartney

Key of G

Intro

Moderately fast

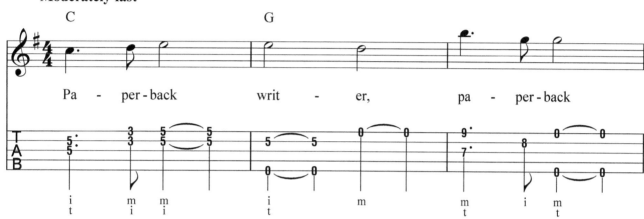

Pa - per-back   writ - er,   pa - per-back

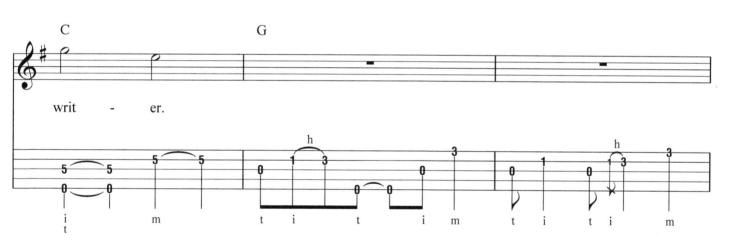

writ - er.

1. Dear

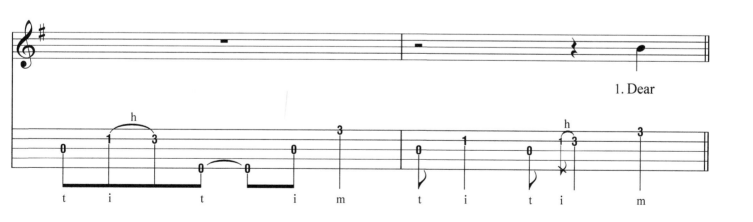

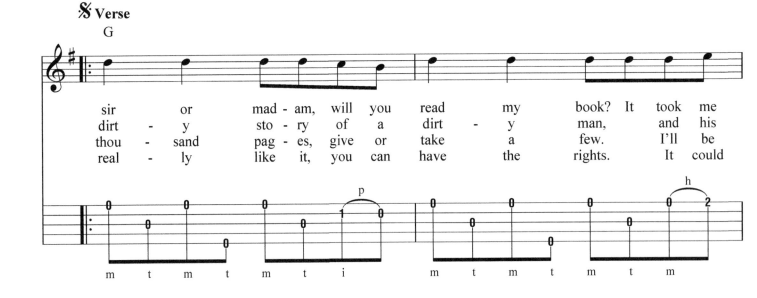

sir or mad - am, will you read my book? It took me
dirt - y sto - ry of a dirt - y man, and his
thou - sand pag - es, give or take a few. I'll be
real - ly like it, you can have the rights. It could

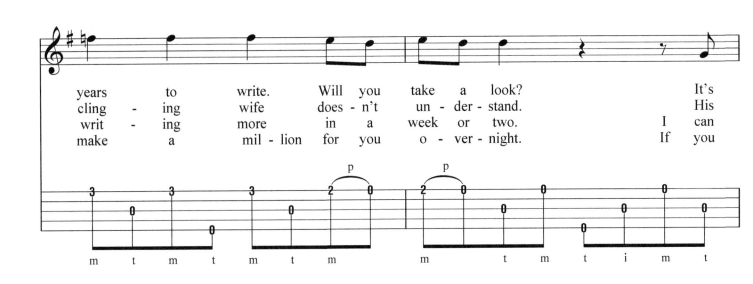

years to write. Will you take a look? It's
cling - ing wife does - n't un - der - stand. His
writ - ing more in a week or two. I can
make a mil - lion for you o - ver - night. If you

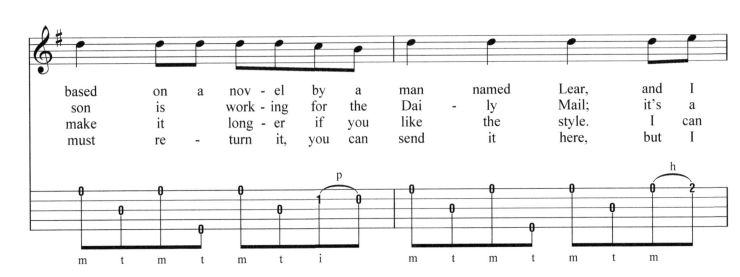

based on a nov - el by a man named Lear, and I
son is work - ing for the Dai - ly Mail; it's a
make it long - er if you like the style. I can
must re - turn it, you can send it here, but I

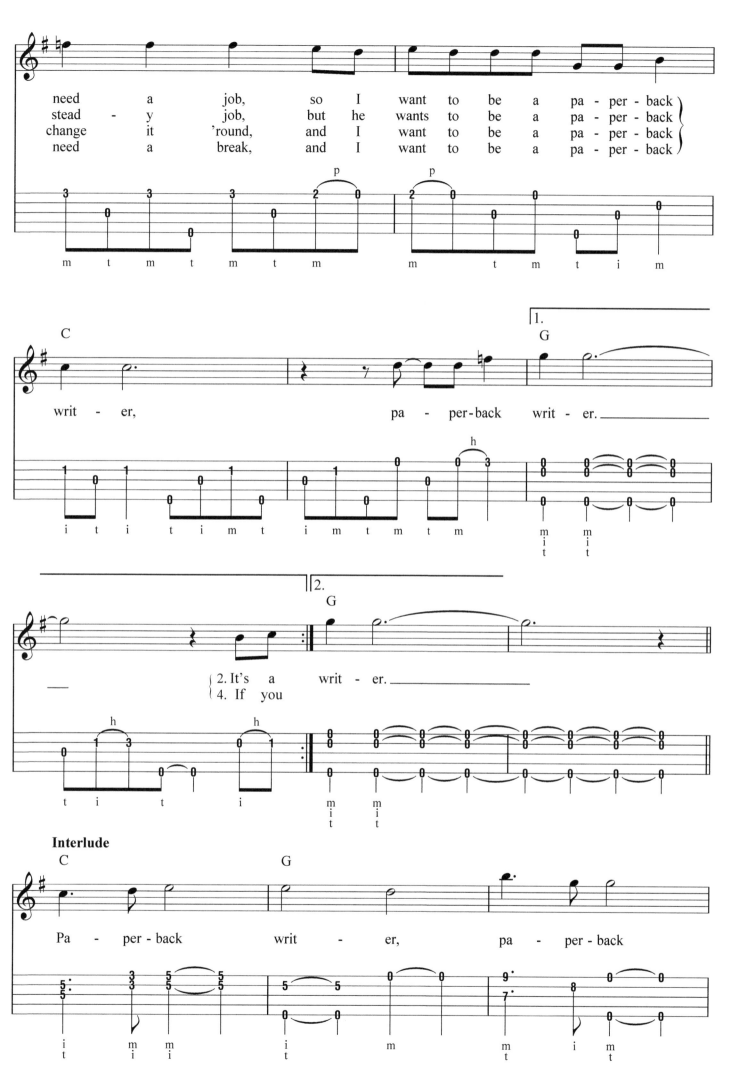

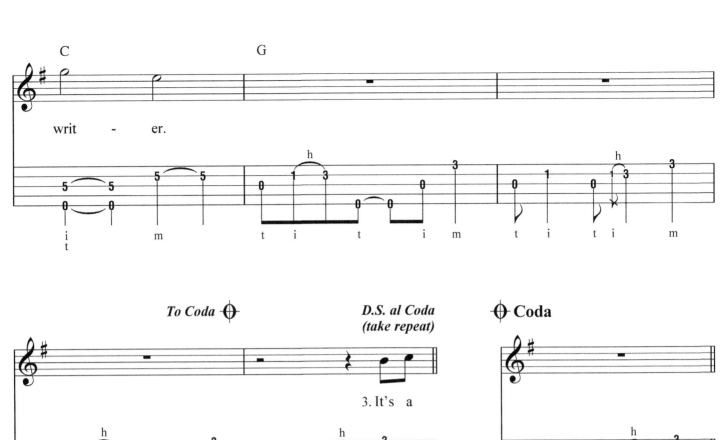

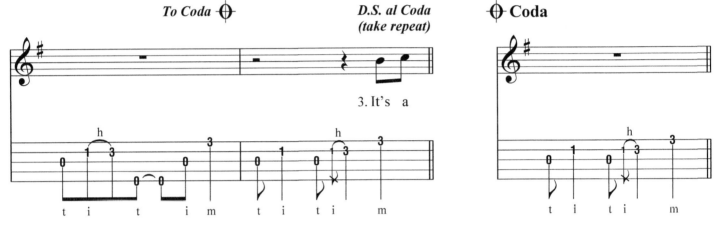

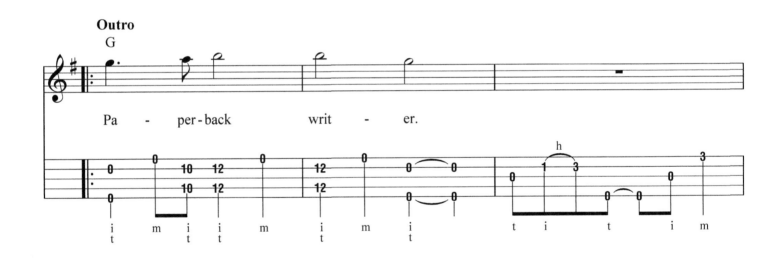

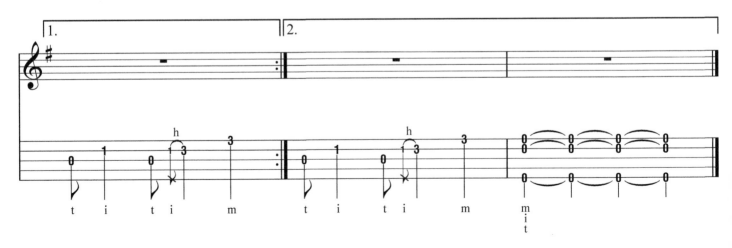

Nowhere Man

Words and Music by John Lennon and Paul McCartney

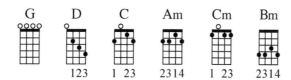

Key of G

Verse

Moderately

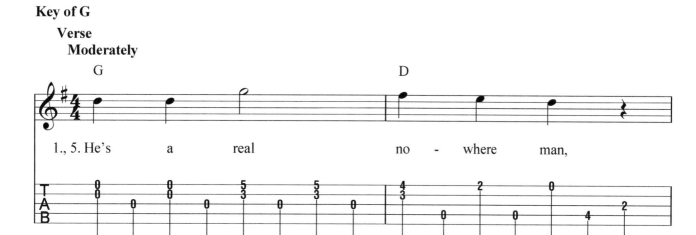

1., 5. He's a real no - where man,

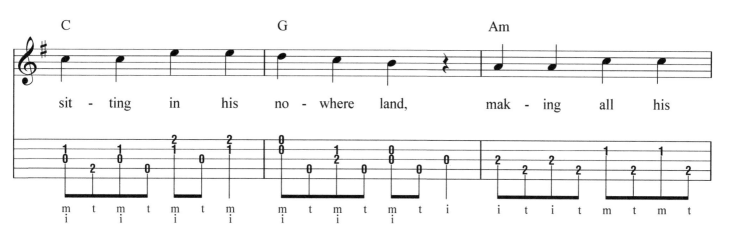

sit - ting in his no - where land, mak - ing all his

To Coda ⊕

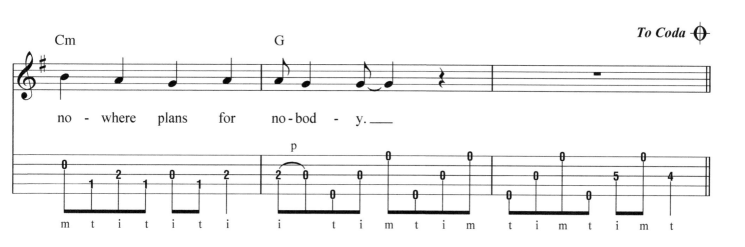

no - where plans for no - bod - y. ___

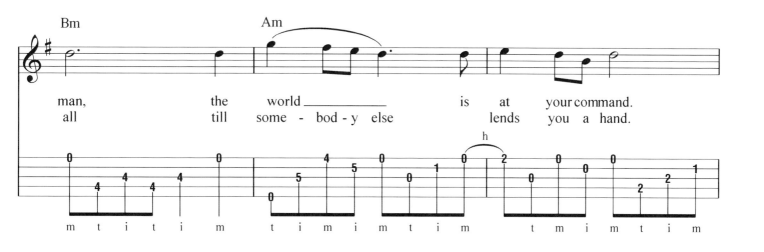

man,   the   world _____ is   at   your command.
all   till   some - bod - y else   lends   you a hand.

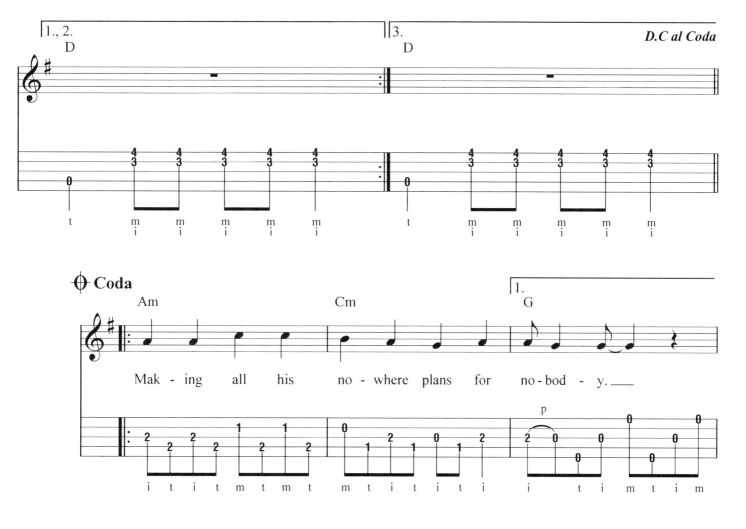

Making all his no - where plans for no - bod - y. _____

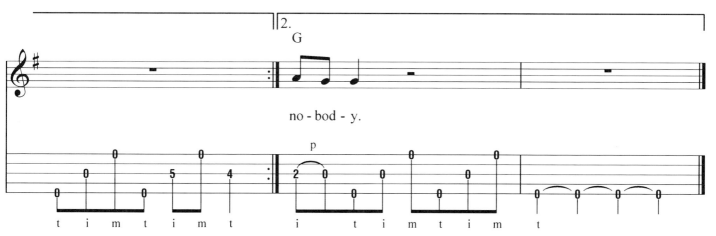

no - bod - y.

BANJO NOTATION LEGEND

TABLATURE graphically represents the banjo fingerboard. Each horizontal line represents a string, and each number represents a fret.

4th string, 2nd fret   1st & 2nd strings open, played together

TIME SIGNATURE:
The upper number indicates the number of beats per measure, the lower number indicates that a quarter note gets one beat.

CUT TIME:
Each note's time value should be cut in half. As a result, the music will be played twice as fast as it is written.

QUARTER NOTE:
time value = 1 beat

EIGHTH NOTES:
time value = 1/2 beat each

single   in series

SIXTEENTH NOTES:
time value = 1/4 beat each

single   in series

DOTTED QUARTER NOTE:
time value = 1 1/2 beat

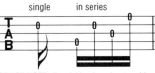

TIE: Pick the 1st note only, then let it sustain for the combined time value.

TRIPLET: Three notes played in the same time normally occupied by two notes of the same time value.

GRACE NOTE: A quickly played note with no time value of its own. The grace note and the note following it only occupy the time value of the second note.

RITARD: A gradual slowing of the tempo or speed of the song.

QUARTER REST:
time value = 1 beat of silence

EIGHTH REST:
time value = 1/2 beat of silence

HALF REST:
time value = 2 beats of silence

WHOLE REST:
time value = 4 beats of silence

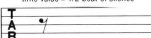
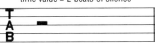
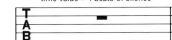

ENDINGS: When a repeated section has a first and second ending, play the first ending only the first time and play the second ending only the second time.

REPEAT SIGNS: Play the music between the repeat signs two times.

D.S. AL CODA:
Play through the music until you complete the measure labeled *"D.S. al Coda,"* then go back to the sign (%).
Then play until you complete the measure labeled *"To Coda ⊕,"* then skip to the section labeled *" ⊕ Coda."*

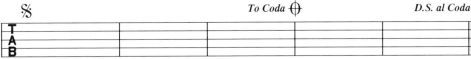

HAMMER-ON: Strike the first (lower) note with one finger, then sound the higher note (on the same string) with another finger by fretting it without picking.

PULL-OFF: Place both fingers on the notes to be sounded. Strike the first note and without picking, pull the finger off to sound the second (lower) note.

SLIDE UP: Strike the first note and then slide the same fret-hand finger up to the second note. The second note is not struck.

SLIDE DOWN: Strike the first note and then slide the same fret-hand finger down to the second note. The second note is not struck.

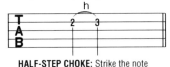
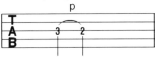
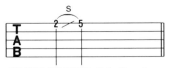

HALF-STEP CHOKE: Strike the note and bend the string up 1/2 step.

WHOLE-STEP CHOKE: Strike the note and bend the string up one step.

NATURAL HARMONIC: Strike the note while the fret-hand lightly touches the string directly over the fret indicated.

BRUSH: Play the notes of the chord indicated by quickly rolling them from bottom to top.

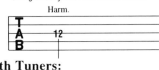

Scruggs/Keith Tuners:

HALF-TWIST UP: Strike the note, twist tuner up 1/2 step, and continue playing.

HALF-TWIST DOWN: Strike the note, twist tuner down 1/2 step, and continue playing.

WHOLE-TWIST UP: Strike the note, twist tuner up one step, and continue playing.

WHOLE-TWIST DOWN: Strike the note, twist tuner down one step, and continue playing.

Right Hand Fingerings

t = thumb   i = index finger   m = middle finger